This book's message is  the answers it gives an what multitudes today ㅤ ㅤ ㅤ —and seemingly unable to find on their own. It is fitting that Darrell and Virgil would write about how to rise above our fears, because they are two of the most intrepid, unflinching, stout-hearted men I have ever had the privilege of knowing. They have written this book with their characteristic courage and raw clarity, and I know you will be blessed by it.

Phil Johnson
Executive director
Grace to You

What a timely resource. *Why Are You Afraid?* will encourage so many in this hour of anxiety. Sometimes fear paralyzes us from living boldly in our faith or causes defeat when we should really be living testimonies of the power of God. I'm so thankful for the courage of Darrell Harrison and Virgil Walker, and this book will help you understand the source of fear and the path to overcoming fear in your daily life.

Brad Jurkovich, DMin
Senior Pastor
First Baptist Church – Bossier City, LA
Conservative Baptist Network, Spokesman

The most oft-repeated command in the Bible is, "Do not fear." The events of the past couple of years give every indication that such repetition is warranted. Evidently, entire nations can be brought to their knees without firing a shot, so long as tyrants can keep people in a perpetual state of fear. Whether it's the fear of sickness and death, of being called a racist, or of being canceled for questioning the narrative of politically-correct secularism, the enemies of righteousness seem to have successfully weaponized fear. That means the people of God need to be equipped to stand against this manipulation and battle the temptation to be sinfully fearful. *Why Are You So Afraid?* is a helpful tool for just that. Faithfully expounding the relevant Scriptures, Darrell and Virgil give the church a battle plan to stand firm against the attacks of the enemy, preeminently by holding forth the truth of God and calling Christians to act faith upon His promises. Read and be blessed.

Michael Riccardi, PhD
Assistant Professor of Theology
The Master's Seminary
Pastor of Local Outreach Ministries
Grace Community Church

Why Are You Afraid? is a much-needed resource on the subject of anxiety. It is thorough, careful, balanced, biblically precise, and introduces the reader to many other faithful voices, down through the ages, who also bring the reader to the Word of God. I am thankful for this fine work and recommend it joyfully.

Richard Caldwell, DMin
Pastor-Teacher
Founders Baptist Church

With an introductory reminder that fear began in the garden (Gn. 3:8) and building upon the poignant question that Jesus asked the disciples in the storm—"Why are you afraid...?" (Mt. 8:26), the authors show us how to address fear. In the midst of the fear and anxiety that is so prominent in our world today, we have a choice as to upon what we focus our minds. Here's the simple, profound truth taught in this volume: the cure for sinful fear and anxiety is a heart-centered trust in God and in his infallible and inerrant Word. Darrell and Virgil do a great job reminding us that God's Word is sufficient to calm our soul, and they provide instruction as to how we can be without fear. This book will be a joyful, yet challenging encouragement to you—I recommend it without hesitation.

John E. Babler, PhD
Professor and Chairman
Department of Biblical Counseling
Mid-America Baptist Seminary
Fellow and Member of the Board of Trustees
Association of Certified Biblical Counselors.

In a day and age full of fear, the need for Christians to be reminded of the necessity to trust God is as great as it has ever been. In this helpful book, Darrell and Virgil build upon the Scriptures and centuries of church history to create a short, accessible book that redirects the Christian away from worldly fears and toward biblical assurance of God's sovereignty.

Becky Aniol, PhD
Educator

Like all their work, Darrell and Virgil's message here is timely, straightforward, unflinchingly biblical, and incredibly hopeful. We can overcome fear. The secular, godless world tries to exchange one lie of fear for another lie of empty philosophies to manage or indulge emotions, attempting to navigate darkness without direction and resulting in misery. If you have suffered under the weight of fear, this book will help you understand how to navigate those lies with the light of Truth, applying the Truth of God to your life and begin to trust Him, exchanging fear for real, lasting peace.

Jenna Ellis, Esq.
Attorney for John MacArthur
and Grace Community Church

After reading this excellent short book, all I can say is: I'm not afraid. That's because Darrell Harrison and Virgil Walker have done in these pages what they do in their epic podcast: they fill me with faith. They douse me in courage. They fire me up to live boldly. These two men are a blessing to the church, and in these pages they show why: they load us up with Scripture, with great quotations from sound men, and they apply the Word searchingly and aggressively. In a world positively paralyzed by fear, these Word-teachers have found the way out. They have picked the lock. They have sprung the trap. The cure to our fear-drenched context is, in a word, Christ. Look to him and live--fearlessly.

Owen Strachan, PhD
Author, *Christianity and Wokeness*
Provost, Grace Bible Theological Seminary

Why Are You Afraid?

Darrell Harrison
Virgil Walker

G3 Press
Douglasville, GA

Why Are You Afraid?

Copyright © 2022 by Darrell Harrison and Virgil Walker

Published by G3 Press
4979 GA-5
Douglasville, GA 30135
www.G3Min.org

All rights reserved. No part of this publication may be repro-
duced, stored in a retrieval system, or transmitted in any form
by any means, electronic, mechanical, photocopy, recording, or
otherwise, without prior permission of the publisher, except as
provided for by USA copyright law.

Unless otherwise noted, Scripture quotations taken from the
(NASB®) New American Standard Bible®, Copyright © 1960,
1971, 1977, 1995, 2020 by The Lockman Foundation. Used by
permission. All rights reserved. www.lockman.org.

Printed in the United States of America

ISBN: 979-8-9855187-0-2

Cover Design: Joe Zarate

Contents

Foreword

Among all the creatures God hath made
(devils only excepted) man is the most apt and able to be
his own tormentor; and of all the scourges with which he
lasheth and afflicteth both his mind and body,
none is found so cruel and intolerable
as his own fears.[1]
—John Flavel

The familiar lyrics from the hymn "How Firm a Foundation" is a call to faith:

Fear not, I am with you,
O be not dismayed,
for I am your God
and will still give you aid;
I'll strengthen you, help you,
and cause you to stand,
upheld by my righteous,
omnipotent hand.

This is a direct quote from Isaiah 41:10. The children of God are given the command in Scripture to trust God in all circumstances. A lack of trust

---

[1] John Flavel, *A Practical Treatise on Fear*, in *The Whole Works of John Flavel*, vol. 3 (London: W. Baynes and Son, 1820), 239.

in God is a demonstration of a shallow faith. We see this put on vivid display when the disciples are moved to terror in the midst of a storm at sea.

While the waves were spilling over into the boat, they failed to consider that the Creator of the wind and waves was also in the boat with them. This is a lesson they would soon learn, but only after they had the audacity to rebuke Jesus for the fact that he was asleep and unmoved by their circumstances. Jesus responded with some piercing and sobering words, "Why are you afraid, O you of little faith" (Matt 8:26).

Fear is spoken of in Scripture in both a positive and negative form. After a life of pleasure and pain, Solomon writes, "The end of the matter; all has been heard. Fear God and keep his commandments, for this is the whole duty of man" (Ecc 12:13). Everything else, according to Solomon, is "vanity of vanities." With all of Solomon's wisdom, he also collected scars from the empty pursuits of life. To reverence and honor God is our calling, making the fear of God a good thing.

In the New Testament, we find the common word *phobeō* used to describe people who are in a state of fear or terror. It is from this Greek term that the English word *phobia* finds its origin. We see this term used in a powerful way in Jesus's instruction on fear in Matthew 10:28:

> And do not fear those who kill the body but cannot kill the soul. Rather fear him who can destroy both soul and body in hell. (ESV)

Every single day there are many things that could happen to us at any given moment that could negatively impact our life or even cause our death. Sadly, many people awake every morning crippled by such possibilities and it drives them to despair, depression, and in some cases suicide. Consider the list of common phobias that grip people on a daily basis:

Arachnophobia: fear of spiders
Coulrophobia: fear of clowns
Bibliophobia: fear of books
Dentophobia: fear of dentists
Achluophobia: fear of darkness
Porphyrophobia: fear of the color purple
Acrophobia: fear of heights
Anthophobia: fear of flowers
Pyrophobia: fear of fire
Alektorophobia: fear of chickens
Samhainophobia: fear of Halloween

Obesophobia: fear of gaining weight

While most of us have no serious fear of flowers, chickens, or the color purple, we do perhaps know people who battle with *pathophobia*, which is the fear of disease. We sometimes refer to these people as *hypochondriacs*. Many of us have likewise known someone who struggled with *verminophobia,* and we call this person a *germaphobe* (someone who has a fear of germs). Perhaps the most common fear that plagues people in general is *thanatophobia* which is the fear of death. This is a compound term that combines the Greek term *thanatos* (meaning death) with *phobia* (meaning to be afraid, fearful, or terrified). Yet, in Scripture, we are given the command to put our trust in the Lord and to avoid such cultural fear and anxiety.

If the creator of life holds our very next breath, why would we be gripped and controlled by fearful circumstances that are beyond our ability to foresee or manage? Really the question comes down to whether we trust God to manage the affairs of life. The circumstances of life include the laws of nature, depraved human hearts, wicked politicians, small spiders, car accidents, disease, and death. Such circumstances include both large and visible public policies and microscopic airborne illnesses. Is this our Father's world? Does he rule over all things? We look at this broken world and expect unbelievers to fear, but why is the church afraid?

One of the most helpful passages of Scripture on this subject is found in the sermon on the mount in Matthew 6. In this passage, Jesus makes the clear case that if God provides for the birds of the air and the lilies of the field, how much more does God love and care for his people. Jesus moves to a climactic point where he says, "But seek first the kingdom of God and his righteousness, and all these things will be added to you" (Matt 6:33). Our God remains faithful, and we must learn to trust him in all circumstances.

As the world continues to turn, it is inevitable that we will continue to be shocked by breaking news that will have an impact upon us as individuals and our local churches. We will all experience that dreaded phone call that informs us of the death of a dear friend or a loved one. Yet, we must learn to live life in a spirit of joy as opposed to crippling fear of the unknown circumstances that might plague us tomorrow. As the Puritan John Flavel once said, "Either we know not, or at least do not duly consider his almighty power, vigilant care, unspotted faithfulness, and how they are all engaged, by covenant, for his people."[2] As the Psalmist David writes, our God is our Rock and our Deliverer and it's in him that we place our trust (Ps 18:2).

Darrell Harrison and Virgil Walker are more than cultural commentators who analyze the critical social justice movement through the lens of Scripture. They are skilled students of God's word who love the church and desire to equip God's people with the truths of Scripture. In this book, they not only identify the root problem of fear, they likewise direct us to the source of all joy through the gospel hope that we share in Christ. It is my joy to commend this book to you and one that I believe would be an accessible resource for the Christian home, the pastor's office, and the church library.

It is a joy to call Darrell Harrison and Virgil Walker friends. Not only do they take the faith seriously, but they're also unafraid to take

---

[2] John Flavel, *A Practical Treatise of Fear*, 258.

unpopular stands in the public sphere. In this cancel culture atmosphere within our society, we need faithful men to stand firm, and these brothers are fine examples of what it means to speak the truth even when it's not the popular thing to communicate.

If you've listened to the Just Thinking Podcast with Darrell Harrison and Virgil Walker, you know they take the faith seriously and approach each subject with theological precision and helpful application. That very same approach is communicated in their book, and I pray that this book will be an encouragement to you as you journey onward in the faith.

Josh Buice
Pastor of Pray's Mill Baptist Church
Founder and President of G3 Ministries

Acknowledgments

First and foremost, I would like to thank my Lord and Savior Jesus Christ for mercifully redeeming such a wretched sinner as myself (Rom 5:6). I'd also like to thank Dr. John MacArthur for his spiritual leadership and counsel, as well as Phil Johnson, Jay Flowers, Bill Fickett, Jeremiah Johnson, and the staff and volunteers of Grace to You, for encouraging and supporting me in such ministry endeavors as this book. I could not have done it without you.

Darrell

I continue to be humbled by the way God chooses to use the weak and foolish for his glory, for which I will be eternally grateful. I want to thank my wife, Tomeka, for her consistent prayerful support and encouragement; there's no more incredible cheerleader. The support I've received from men like John Babler and Dale Johnson in Biblical Counseling has been foundational to my understanding of the sufficiency of Scripture on these matters. I would also thank the leadership team at G3 Ministries, Josh Buice and Scott Aniol, for their work and support on this project.

Virgil

Introduction

The subject of this book is what the Word of God has to say about sinful fear and anxiety. We say *sinful* fear and anxiety because we believe there is an important distinction to be made between illegitimate and legitimate fear. We'll endeavor to examine those distinctions later, but suffice it to say that not all fear and anxiety is sinful in and of itself.

One of the manifestations of God's common grace in the world is that embedded within each of us as his image-bearers (Gen 1:27) is an element of fear and anxiety that is healthy — "healthy" in the sense that when one considers that we live in a world that has been corrupted by sin (Rom 8:9-21), there are occasions when expressions of fear or anxiety are entirely right and proper.

For example, let's say you wake up tomorrow morning and find that there's a brown recluse spider on your pillow. In such a situation, we would suggest that you have every right to be fearful because of your awareness that brown recluse spiders are among some of the most venomous spiders in the world. There are other examples, of course, but the point we're trying to make is perhaps better reflected in these words from Stuart Scott:

> There is a fear of danger and difficult circumstances that is reasonable. We would not be living in reality if we did not even consider how an upcoming situation might affect us. God wants us to live in reality, but at the same time he wants us to bring him into the picture. It is reasonable to respond to danger and disaster. God has equipped us with a bodily response — an increase in adrenaline production — that can help us when physical danger is imminent. This increase can cause other bodily responses: pounding heart, muscle tension, heightened awareness, dry mouth, perspiration, and butterflies of the stomach. As long as we do not let our fear or our feelings keep us from doing what is right, and we turn to God in our fear, that fear is not ungodly. We are all going to feel afraid sometimes. But don't make the mistake of equating courage with a lack of feeling afraid. The most courageous Christians are those who feel afraid but who, when they feel afraid, place their trust in God and do what he says to do. The question is: what do we *do* when we are afraid? "When I am afraid,

I will put my trust in You" (Ps 56:3).[3]

Furthermore, it's essential to identify the difference between godly fear like that found in Proverbs 9:10 ("The fear of the Lord is the beginning of wisdom, and the knowledge of the Holy One is understanding.") and the fear of man like Jesus describes in Matthew 10:28 ("Do not fear those who kill the body but are unable to kill the soul; but rather fear him who is able to destroy both soul and body in hell.").

With those important distinctions in mind, we should set some expectations for what this book is not.

This book on sinful fear and anxiety should not be regarded as an exhaustive treatment of that subject, nor is this short book intended to address every conceivable situation imaginable in which a believer might experience sinful fear and anxiety. This book won't tell you how you should respond in every circumstance because such instances are unique to each individual. The subject of fear and anxiety is so broad that

---

[3] Stuart Scott, *Anger, Anxiety, and Fear: A Biblical Perspective* (Bemidji, MN: Focus Publishing, 2009), 15.

there is no possible way to address every single area of life in which someone can experience fear.

Our goal in this book is simply to provide some biblical precepts from God's Word concerning sinful fear and anxiety and to encourage believers to take those principles to heart and apply them in their own lives. Our heart's desire for people who are reading this book is echoed quite well in these words from the seventeenth-century English Puritan, John Owen:

> O that we might advise one another as to what to do; to help one another to recover from our weaknesses! This is what we are called to, what is required of us: to have faith in the faithfulness of Christ who has built his church upon the rock so that however bad things might be, nothing will prevail against it; to have faith in the fullness of the Spirit and Christ's promise to send him to renew the face of the church; to have faith in apprehending the truth of God, who has foretold these things; and to have a faith that stirs us up to attend to those special duties that God requires at our hands at such a time.[4]

---

[4] John Owen, *Searching Our Hearts in Difficult Times* (Carlisle, PA: Banner of Truth, 2019), 144.

That is our desire and prayer for this book, that God would grant us his wisdom so that we might be able to "advise" our brothers and sisters struggling with sinful fear and anxiety. We hope to help believers to, as John Owen said, "recover from their weaknesses" — and we all have weaknesses — every one of us. As David Powlison writes,

The darkness of the human condition is characterized by two immense wrongs that create turmoil throughout our lives: a complex mix of moral evils arises from inside us; a complex mix of situational evils besets us. The Bible uses the word *evil* to describe both sin and suffering, just as we do in English. Something *inside* us is wrong. People believe, think, feel, want, and do bad things. Of course, the obvious atrocities are moral evils. But the falsity, self-deception, and godlessness of "normal" life and the misshapenness of "normal" desires similarly count as moral evil in God's assessment. We are "off," in relation to both God and other people. And things *outside* us are wrong. Bad things happen to us. Other people betray us. We face losses, sicknesses, and death. We swim in the falsehoods of our sociocultural milieu. A Liar and Murderer [meaning Satan] is out to deceive and kill us. In sum, we face troubles (externally); we are troublesome (interpersonally); and we are troubled (psychologically), struggling both with what we face and with who we are.[5]

Powlison says we struggle both with what we face and with who we are. That's very true. But even so, thanks be to God that his elect can rely on these comforting and reassuring words from Psalm 103:14: "For he himself knows our frame; he is mindful that we are but dust."

Yes, some fear is justified; however, today's culture seems to peddle in fear. Just take a quick look through the front page of any major media outlet, and what you'll find is an endless parade of fear as headline news.

For example, one recent look at CNN.com showed the following news stories:

"Earthquake strikes near Haiti."

Another said, "Antarctica is melting. Its future could be catastrophic."

Finally, here's a story taking direct aim at fear: "'Still people have fear.' What life is like in

---

[5] David Powlison, *How Does Sanctification Work?* (Wheaton, IL: Crossway, 2017), 66–67.

some cities captured by the Taliban."

Here in the U.S., we have everything from CRT to COVID, to Socialist Communism on the rise. All of this creates a tremendous amount of anxiety and fear.

It's time for us to address this topic with biblical clarity.

Study Questions

1. Why is it important to properly discern between *legitimate* and *illegitimate* fear and anxiety?

2. Read Proverbs 9:10 and Matthew 10:28. Why is the understanding of "the fear of the Lord" an important baseline when addressing the issue of fear?

3. Read 1 Thessalonians 5:21. What are some potential spiritual pitfalls of not "carefully examining" your fears and anxieties in light of what Scripture teaches?

4. In what way(s), if at all, did the quote by Stuart Scott (p. 2) impact and challenge you?

5. In the quote by David Powlison (p. 6) what are the two things he identifies that "create turmoil" in our lives?

6. In what ways have you witnessed our culture peddle in sinful fear and anxiety?

The Roots of Sinful Fear

The first account of fear and anxiety in human history is found in Genesis 3:8–10 and the account of the fall of mankind into sin:

> [Adam and Eve] heard the sound of the Lord God walking in the garden in the cool of the day, and the man and his wife hid themselves from the presence of the Lord God among the trees of the garden. Then the Lord God called to the man, and said to him, "Where are you?" He said, "I heard the sound of You in the garden, and I was afraid because I was naked; so I hid myself."

Notice what compelled Adam and Eve to hide from God: fear. Of course, having sinned against a holy and righteous God, Adam and Eve had every reason to be in dread in that moment. But listen to what John Calvin has to say about their reaction:

> Although this seems to be the confession of a dejected and humbled man, it will nevertheless soon appear that he was not yet properly subdued, nor led to repentance. He imputes his fear to the voice of God, and to his own nakedness, as if he had never before heard God speaking

without being alarmed, and had not been even sweetly exhilarated by his speech. His excessive stupidity appears in this that he fails to recognize the cause of shame in his sin; he, therefore, shows that he does not yet so feel his punishment, as to confess his fault. In the meantime, he proves what I said before to be true, that original sin does not reside in one part of the body only, but holds its dominion over the whole man, and so occupies every part of the soul, that none remains in its integrity; for, notwithstanding his fig-leaves, he still dreads the presence of God.[6]

Calvin's words should prompt us to examine our own hearts to determine if the fear and anxiety we may be experiencing isn't in fact rooted in some sin in our lives we've refused to resolve truthfully with God. In other words, like Adam and Eve, we've covered our sins with fig leaves, so to speak, instead of genuinely confessing them and turning away from them in our hearts.

If we find that we do not believe, we must simply repent and believe. As R. C. Sproul, Jr. writes,

---

[6] John Calvin, *Commentary on the First Book of Moses Called Genesis*, trans. John King, vol. 1 (Bellingham, WA: Logos Bible Software, 2010), 162.

What do we do about our unbelief? The same thing we do with all our sins, which are, in the end, unbelief. We repent and believe the gospel. When we grumble, and we all do, we must turn from our grumbling and cry out for his mercy. Then we must believe that when we confess our sins, he is faithful and just to forgive us our sins and to cleanse us from all unrighteousness [1 John 1:9]. No enemy can stop him from cleansing us from all unrighteousness, for he already has overcome the world [John 16:33]. So let us believe, and let us be of good cheer.[7]

Scripture is clear — we must turn away from our sins. Sometimes Christians have the idea that since we have been eternally forgiven, we need no longer repent of our sins. British theologian A. W. Pink addresses this wrong thinking:

Every privilege of the gospel entails an added obligation upon its recipient. As creatures — it is our bounden duty to be in entire subjection to our Creator. As new creatures in Christ — it doubly behooves us to serve God cheerfully. It is a great mistake to suppose that grace sets aside the claims of righteousness, or that the Law of God

---

[7] R. C. Sproul, Jr., *Believing God* (Lake Mary, FL: Reformation Trust Publishing, 2009), 111.

demands less from the *saved* than it does from the *unsaved*.[8]

As professing believers in Jesus Christ, each of us would do well to *consistently* examine ourselves to ensure that our hearts are right before God and that there is no unconfessed sin in our lives, so that our fellowship with him is not broken. Each of us should echo the words of the prophet Jeremiah: "But You know me, O Lord; You see me; and You examine my heart's attitude toward You" (Jer 12:3a). The psalmist wrote, "If I regard wickedness in my heart, the Lord will not hear" (Ps 66:18). If we hide sin in our hearts, no wonder our hearts are filled with fear and anxiety.

We will quote from several Puritans on this subject particularly because these men suffered quite a bit of religious persecution, and yet they remained faithfully committed to Scripture and rested in the sovereignty of God amid challenging circumstances. During the seventeenth century, nearly twenty thousand Puritans emigrated to the New World because of the

---

[8] Arthur W. Pink, *Pink Jewels* (Lafayette, IN: Sovereign Grace Publishers, 2001), 117.

persecution they were enduring.

You can witness the confidence in God these men displayed simply by reading their prayers. One of the factors that led to such confidence in God was that these men understood their lowliness as compared to the sovereignty of God, which further caused them to rest in him despite persecution. They knew that unconfessed sin would prevent them from fully resting in God amid persecution. For example, in a prayer titled "Sin" in *The Valley of Vision*, one Puritan prayed,

> Merciful Lord, pardon all my sins of this day, week, year, all the sins of my life, sins of early, middle, and advanced years, of omission and commission, of morose, peevish, and angry tempers, of lip, life and walk, of hard-heartedness, unbelief, presumption, pride, of unfaithfulness to the souls of men, of want of bold decision in the cause of Christ, of deficiency in outspoken zeal for his glory, of bringing dishonour upon Thy great name, of deception, injustice, untruthfulness in my dealings with others, of impurity in thought, word, and deed, of covetousness, which is idolatry, of substance unduly hoarded, improvidently squandered, not consecrated to the glory of Thee, the great Giver; sins in private and in the family, in study and recreation, in the

busy haunts of men, in the study of thy Word and in the neglect of it, in prayer irreverently offered and coldly withheld, in time misspent, in yielding to Satan's wiles, in opening my heart to his temptations, in being unwatchful when I know him nigh, in quenching the Holy Spirit; sins against light and knowledge, sins against conscience and the restraints of thy Spirit, sins against the law of eternal love. Pardon all my sins, known and unknown, felt and unfelt, confessed and not confessed, remembered or forgotten. Good Lord, hear; and hearing, forgive.[9]

This kind of reflection and repentance followed by the light of the gospel should be of relief to the sinner. Why? Because God, the righteous judge, has forgiven you. When we have too high a view of our own self-importance, we begin to worry about the things over which we have no control.

Compare that prayer (and its focus) to this prayer by a famous evangelical preacher today:

I declare I will speak only positive words of faith and victory over myself, my family, and my

---

[9] Arthur Bennett, ed., *The Valley of Vision: A Collection of Puritan Prayers & Devotions* (Carlisle, PA: Banner of Truth, 1975), 87.

future. I will not use my words to describe the situation. I will use my words to change my situation. I will call in favor, good breaks, healing, and restoration. I will not talk to God about how big my problems are. I will talk to my problems about how big my God is. This is my declaration. . . . In Jesus's name, Amen.

While the first prayer is to a sovereign God with an understanding of one's position in the world as a fallen sinner, the second is a prayer to oneself (as God). Anytime you're praying about what you will declare or decree and use "in Jesus's name" at the end of it, you're engaged in language more akin to a magic spell than a prayer to God.

The point is this: we often find ourselves worrying because we don't truly depend on God. We are strictly relying on ourselves. The source of much of our sinful fear and anxiety is that we think far too much of ourselves. Can you imagine how little our concern would be for the world if we would focus on our own need for repentance before a Holy God? Instead, we often act as if *we* are at the center of our universe, and we must order all things accordingly. Like the Puritans, if we listened to and obeyed Scripture, we would shift our focus more properly toward God.

Matthew 6:33 gives us a simple truth: "But seek first His kingdom and his righteousness, and all these things will be added to you." Setting your eyes upon God will remind you of your sinful condition, will cause you to repent, and will create the conditions in which you can fully rest in God and his grace.

Study Questions

1. Read Genesis 3:8–10. Why do you think Adam was "afraid" (v. 10)? Have you ever tried to hide from the presence of God because of your own sin? What lesson(s) did you learn from those situations?

2. To what degree has unbelief in God and in His Word factored into the sinful fear and anxiety you've experienced in your walk with Christ?

3. Did you find the quote from R. C. Sproul, Jr. (p. 11) encouraging? If so, why? If not, why?

4. In what way does the Puritan writer's prayer on sin (p. 13) help to provide a correct view of yourself and your relation to God?

5. What are some practical ways you can apply Matthew 6:33 to your struggle with sinful fear and anxiety?

6. In what ways can a healthy prayer life help you to refrain from sinful fear and anxiety?

Why Are You Afraid?

Remember God

Employees in the Department of the Treasury become so proficient at recognizing counterfeit currency because they spend countless hours studying the real thing. Likewise, when you learn to recognize what legitimate fear and anxiety actually are, you're then able to distinguish between that and sinful fear and anxiety. Only then will you be able to respond biblically.

It is an unfortunate reality that most people, including many professing Christians, define fear and anxiety through the subjective lens of their own circumstantial experiences, as opposed to through the objective and fixed lens of the Word of God. Puritan John Flavel observed,

> There is as much diversity in people's inward moods and dispositions as in their outward features. Some are as frightened as rabbits and jump at every sound—even a dog's bark. Some are as bold as lions and face danger without trembling. Some fear more than they ought, and others when they ought not at all. The carnal person fears man, not God. The strong Christian fears God, not man. The weak Christian fears man too much and God too little. There is a fear which is

the effect of sin. It springs from guilt and hurries the soul into more guilt. There is a fear which is the effect of grace. It springs from our love to God and his interest and drives the soul to him in the way of duty. The less fear a person has, the more happiness he has—unless, of course, it is that fear which is his happiness and his excellence. . . . It cannot be said of any person, as it is said of Leviathan: he is "made without fear" (Job 41:33b). The strongest people are not without some fears. When the church is in the storms of persecution, and almost covered with the waves, her most courageous passengers may suffer as much from the boisterous passion within as from the storm without. This is the result of not thoroughly believing or seasonably remembering that the Lord—Admiral of all the oceans and Commander of all the winds—is on board the ship to steer it and preserve it from the storm."[10]

Flavel's use of the phrase "seasonably remembering" is intriguing. It is often in those "seasons" of trial and adversity that many professing Christians tend to succumb to sinful fear and anxiety in their life. And it's in these types of "seasons," as Flavel said, that many

---

[10] John Flavel, *Triumphing Over Sinful Fear* (Grand Rapids: Reformation Heritage Books, 2011), 1–2.

professing Christians tend to forget that the Lord is "on board the ship to steer it and preserve it from the storm." In fact, Flavel might have had Matthew 8:23–27 in mind when he penned those words:

> When [Jesus] got into the boat, his disciples followed Him. 24 And behold, there arose a great storm on the sea, so that the boat was being covered with the waves; but Jesus himself was asleep. 25 And they came to him and woke him, saying, "Save us, Lord; we are perishing!" 26 He said to them, "Why are you afraid, you men of little faith?" Then he got up and rebuked the winds and the sea, and it became perfectly calm. 27 The men were amazed, and said, "What kind of a man is this, that even the winds and the sea obey him?"

Of course, from this very biblical event is where we took the title of our book, *Why Are You Afraid?* For the Christian, this matter of sinful fear and anxiety is fundamentally a matter of what we allow into our minds and, more specifically, what we *choose* to allow our minds to dwell on as a replacement or substitute for the truth of the Word of God. Consider the following passages:

Philippians 4:6a: Be anxious for nothing.

2 Timothy 1:7: For God has not given us a spirit of timidity, but of power and love and discipline.

Matthew 6:34: So do not worry about tomorrow; for tomorrow will care for itself. Each day has enough trouble of its own.

Matthew 10:28a: Do not fear those who kill the body but are unable to kill the soul.

Those verses are just some of the Scriptures that are easy enough for us to memorize and recall when things are going well for us in life. But when some unexpected or unanticipated difficulty or trial providentially interrupts our lives, those verses—and the truths they contain—suddenly aren't so easy for us to recall. It is exactly in unanticipated circumstances that we actually have to put those truths to work by faith.

It is easy to be like Jesus until you have to be like Jesus.

But as followers of Jesus Christ, what we must remember in those instances is that those situations are all providentially ordained and orchestrated by God himself. As Ecclesiastes 7:14 states, "In the day of prosperity be happy, but in the day of adversity consider—God has made the one as well as the other." If you can get these words firmly and deeply embedded in your mind and heart, you'll never have a bad day. Never.

And yet, considering the exhortation we have in Ecclesiastes to remember that "God has made the one as well as the other," the question for us becomes this: when we are overcome with sensations of fear and anxiety, what are we choosing to remember in those moments? What are we choosing to set the focus of our minds on? The truth is that whatever you choose to set your mind on in those moments when you're feeling fearful and anxious is precisely the thing that is going to guide and direct you in those moments. Ed Welch notes,

> Any time you love or want something deeply, you will notice fear and anxieties because you might not get them. Any time you can't control the fate of those things you want or love, you will

notice fears and anxieties because you might lose them. Good insurance policies might help, but they only lessen the risk on things that aren't our real worries. They can't ensure that our loved ones will outlive us or keep us from the ravages of [old] age. Control and certainty are myths.[11]

As a pastor of mine [Darrell] once said, "The battlefield of Satan is the mind." Seventeenth-century English Puritan, William Gurnall, wrote,

> The fiery darts of Satan which the believing soul is able by faith to quench may be described as of two sorts. First, either those that do pleasingly entice and bewitch with some seeming promises of satisfaction to the creature. Or, second, such as affright and carry horror with them.[12]

Puritan theologian Richard Sibbes has some wise counsel for us concerning guarding our minds against Satan's tactics:

> Are you bruised? Be of good comfort, he calls you. Conceal not your wounds, open all before

---

[11] Edward T. Welch, *Running Scared: Fear, Worry, and the God of Rest* (Greensboro, NC: New Growth Press, 2007), 28.
[12] William Gurnall, *The Christian in Complete Armour* (Carlisle, PA: Banner of Truth, 1964), 76.

him and take not Satan's counsel. Go to Christ, although trembling, as the poor woman who said, "If I may but touch his garment" (Matt 9:21). We shall be healed and have a gracious answer. Go boldly to God in our flesh; he is flesh of our flesh, and bone of our bone for this reason, that we might go boldly to him. Never fear to go to God, since we have such a Mediator with him, who is not only our friend but our brother and husband. . . . Let the world be as it will, if we cannot rejoice in the world, yet we may rejoice in the Lord. His presence makes any condition comfortable.[13]

Did you read that last sentence? Sibbes said that the Lord's presence makes *any* condition comfortable. And yet, despite that truth, how many professing Christians are struggling with sinful fear and anxiety since they are discontent with their present "condition," as Sibbes puts it. Notice what Thomas Boston says:

Is not everyone by nature discontented with his present lot in this world or with some *one* thing or other in it? This also was Adam's case (Gen. 3:5-6). Some *one* thing is always missing so that

---

[13] Richard Sibbes, *The Bruised Reed* (Carlisle, PA: Banner of Truth, 1998), 9.

man is a creature given to changes. And if any doubt this, let them look over all their enjoyments and after a review of them, listen to their own hearts, and they will hear a secret murmuring for want of something, though perhaps if they considered the matter aright, they would see that it is better for them to want than to have that something.[14]

Boston's words remind us of Daniel 3:15–18, where Shadrach, Meshach, and Abed-nego are about to be thrown into the fiery furnace by King Nebuchadnezzar for refusing to worship the golden image he had erected.

"Now if you are ready, at the moment you hear the sound of the horn, flute, lyre, trigon, psaltery, and bagpipe and all kinds of music, to fall down and worship the image I have made, very well. But if you do not worship, you will immediately be cast into the midst of a furnace of blazing fire; and what god is there who can deliver you out of my hands?" Shadrach, Meshach, and Abed-nego replied to the king, "O Nebuchadnezzar, we do not need to give you an answer concerning this matter. If it be so, our God whom we serve is able

[14] Thomas Boston, *Human Nature in Its Fourfold State* (Glasgow: J. & M. Robertson, 1794), 36.

to deliver from the furnace of blazing fire; and he will deliver us out of your hand, O king. But even if he does not, let it be known to you, O king, that we are not going to serve your gods or worship the golden image that you have set up."

That's the kind of spiritual maturity that every professing believer in Christ should aspire to attain—to be so secure in our belief in God and his character that we can say like Shadrach, Meshach, and Abed-nego, even if he does not answer my prayer or resolve this situation in the manner I would like, I'm going to remain faithful to him and trust him nonetheless. This would help our hearts and minds be so at peace in all circumstances, because we have the peace of God which surpasses all human understanding (Phil 4:7).

Study Questions

1. In what way(s) have your emotions contributed to moments of sinful fear and anxiety in your life?

2. John Flavel said, "The weak Christian fears man too much and God too little"

(p. 19). Has the fear of man been an area of weakness for you? If so, why?

3. Read Matthew 10:28. In what way(s) can you apply the exhortation in that verse to your life so as to overcome your fear of man?

4. Read Job 2:9–10 and Ecclesiastes 7:14 and commit them to memory. How does knowing that God providentially ordains situations of adversity in your life deepen your understanding of Him—and of yourself?

5. As you reflect on God's providence in your life, how does this knowledge redirect your fear?

6. Read Matthew 6:34 and memorize it.

Trust God

Sinful fear and anxiety begin in the mind and heart. Craig Troxel, professor of practical theology at Westminster Seminary in California, helpfully explains the importance of understanding the nature of our hearts—our "inner selves":

> Our intellectual life is constantly intrigued with darker musings and deeper motives. Our imagination flirts with reckless fantasies that are rooted in self-indulgence and delusion. Our memories, buried years ago, are conjured up for their revisited pleasure. Our secret thoughts are laced throughout with mischievous designs. None of these are actually seen or heard, but they are all too real. So much of our sin is first conceived by lust, jealousy, bitterness, self-pity, or anger. We pursue these sinful reveries and ambitions with full knowledge that God denounces such evil, even in its contemplation. But we are accountable for what we know, and so much of our sin begins here, in the mind of the heart. . . . The mind, whether fallen or reborn, is always biased, motivated, and impassioned by the state of the heart in general. This should not surprise us. . . . Remember, [the word] "heart" is used in

Scripture, first and foremost, to refer to the unity of our inner self. The mind, the desires, and the will are distinct functions of the heart, but they are not separate or unrelated. They constantly influence and relate to one another. This is the way the heart was meant to operate—with knowledge, affection, and volition working with each other. What the heart enjoys is what the heart will explore. . . . All our knowledge is ethical and has an agenda. The mind is always interpreting.[15]

For the Christian, sinful fear and anxiety is the fruit of a mind that, as Troxel said, is *semper interpretationem*—"always interpreting." Fear and anxiety are a by-product of a mind and heart that have been given over to our sinful flesh instead of a firm trust in God and in his Word.

This raises an important question: In what or in whom are you actually placing your trust? Jerry Bridges notes what is necessary if we are going to rightly place our trust in God alone:

To set the Lord before me is to recognize his

---

[15] A. Craig Troxel, *With All Your Heart: Orienting Your Mind, Desires, and Will toward Christ* (Wheaton, IL: Crossway, 2020), 37–38, 47.

presence and his constant help, but this is something we must choose to do. God is always with
us. He has said, "Never will I leave you; never
will I forsake you" (Hebrews 13:5). There is no
question of his presence with us. But we must
recognize his presence; we must set him always
before us. We must choose whether or not we
will believe his promises of constant protection
and care. . . . We must know that God is sovereign, wise, and loving. . . . But having been ex-
posed to the knowledge of the truth, we must
then choose whether to believe the truth about
God, which he has revealed to us, or whether to
follow our feelings. If we are to trust God, we
must choose to believe his truth. We must say, "I
will trust you though I do not feel like doing
so."[16]

Bridges's final statement raises one of the
most significant impediments to trusting God —
our feelings. Our fickle feelings cause us to dis-
believe the God in whom we've entrusted our
eternal destiny. Consider this: you profess to be
a Christian, someone who, by definition, has entrusted your eternal future to a God you've
never seen, and yet you cannot trust him with

---

[16] Jerry Bridges, *Trusting God* (Colorado Springs: NavPress,
2017), 196–97.

the next five minutes of that situation you're facing?

Richard Caldwell presents the only remedy when he notes,

> When we worry, when we are full of anxiety, what we are dealing with is a pride problem. . . . Until we stop thinking that we handle us better than God handles us, until we stop thinking that he really doesn't know, or [that] he really isn't in control, or [that] he really doesn't care about us— until our minds and hearts change about that, and we put away our pride—we are actually shutting ourselves off from God's help. . . . So the answer to anxiety is as simple as this one word— humility. The problem with the trouble-filled heart is pride. The answer for that pride is repentance. The answer for anxiety is the repentance that recognizes the evil of not trusting God's care for us. It's the repentance of those who choose instead to preach the truth of God's faithfulness to their own hearts and minds.[17]

However, the reality is that we don't often regard fear and anxiety as being sinful to begin

---

[17] Richard Caldwell, *Answering Anxiety: A Biblical Answer for What Troubles Your Heart* (The Woodlands, TX: Kress Christian Publications, 2017), 33–34.

with. In fact, perhaps many professing Christians today consider worry and anxiety as virtuous, having convinced themselves that worrying, especially about someone like a child or a spouse, is evidence that you care deeply about that person. But as Lou Priolo writes,

> If you are a fearful person, you undoubtedly have some idea of how destructive fear can be. It is essential, however, that you understand that above and beyond the misery that sinful fear produces, it is truly offensive to God.[18]

This may be hard to hear, but the biblical reality is that worry, fear, and anxiety are not indicators of care and concern, but are actually indicators of idolatry.

This reminds us of John Calvin's well-known observation: "The human heart is a perpetual idol factory." Scripture clearly and constantly reminds us that we are to fear God; we are not to be afraid of any other circumstance the world has to offer. It's as if Scripture wants to clearly reveal that the expression of fear is only adequately expressed about God. Could it be that

---

[18] Lou Priolo, *Fear: Breaking Its Grip* (Phillipsburg, NJ: P & R Publishing, 2009), 16.

whatever else we might find ourselves fearing, we've elevated to the position that only God holds?

Calvin was right: the current culture is currently engaged in an ever-increasing idolatrous act of self-worship. We see this in everything from selfie culture to gender confusion to the bowed knee at the golden calf of ethnicity. Everything is all about me.

While this is true of culture, it should not be true of the follower of Christ. Our comfort should be found in the understanding of whose we are and that our ultimate end is eternity with Christ.

Scripture commands in Proverbs 3:5–6, "Trust in the Lord with all your heart And do not lean on your own understanding. 6 In all your ways acknowledge Him, And He will make your paths straight." Paul admonishes us in Philippians 4:6, "Do not be anxious about anything, but in everything by prayer and supplication with thanksgiving let your requests be made known to God." To disobey these clear commands is to raise that which we fear to a place that only God should occupy.

The Heidelberg Catechism is helpful in this regard with its first question and answer. This catechism, intended to educate new believers and young people in the faith, contains great comfort. The First Question asks,

What is your only comfort in life and in death?

The catechism answers,

That I am not my own, but belong — body and soul, in life and in death — to my faithful Savior, Jesus Christ.

He has fully paid for all my sins with his precious blood, and has set me free from the tyranny of the devil. He also watches over me in such a way that not a hair can fall from my head without the will of my Father in heaven; in fact, all things must work together for my salvation.

Because I belong to him, Christ, by his Holy Spirit, assures me of eternal life and makes me wholeheartedly willing and ready from now on to live for him.

Study Questions

1. Craig Troxel said, "The mind is always interpreting" (p. 31). What about you? In what way(s) is your mind "always interpreting" so that you become sinfully fearful and anxious about your life?

2. In light of John Calvin's quote, "The human heart is a perpetual idol factory," how have the things you've feared been made an idol?

3. Are you a worrier? If so, make a list of *everything* that you're fearful and anxious about. Be honest and transparent in compiling your list, knowing that God knows your heart (Ps 44:21). Use your list as a means to confess and repent to God for not trusting Him (Mark 9:24).

4. Read Matthew 6:25–34. Make a note of each instance in which Jesus says, "Do not worry." Why do you think Jesus repeated that command as often as He did?

5. Read Matthew 6:8 along with Matthew 6:25–34. Commit Matthew 6:8 to memory. Knowing that you're not to worry because God knows what your needs are *before* you ask Him, how can you apply those two passages to your struggle with sinful fear and anxiety? Be specific.

Why Are You Afraid?

The Word Is Sufficient

In 1 Peter 4:12–13, the apostle Peter gives us this exhortation: "Beloved, do not be surprised at the fiery ordeal among you, which comes upon you for your testing, as though some strange thing were happening to you; but to the degree that you share the sufferings of Christ, keep on rejoicing, so that also at the revelation of his glory you may rejoice with exultation." Paul writes,

> But we have this treasure in earthen vessels, so that the surpassing greatness of the power will be of God and not from ourselves; we are afflicted in every way, but not crushed; perplexed, but not despairing; persecuted, but not forsaken; struck down, but not destroyed; carrying about in the body the dying of Jesus, so that the life of Jesus also may be manifested in our body. For we who live are constantly being delivered over to death for Jesus' sake, so that the life of Jesus also may be manifested in our mortal flesh. . . . For all things are for your sakes, so that the grace which is spreading to more and more people may cause the giving of thanks to abound to the glory of God. (2 Cor 4:7–11, 15)

We must always remember that our circumstances are primarily for the purpose of bringing glory to God, and so we should respond accordingly to whatever comes our way. Unfortunately, we often do not view difficult circumstances this way because we do not have a biblically-informed theology of suffering.

But followers of Christ should expect suffering. Remember what Jesus said to Peter (John 21)? He asked Peter three times, "Do you love me?" Peter's response was, "Yes Lord, I love you, you know all things." And then Jesus said the following to Peter:

> "Truly, truly, I say to you, when you were younger, you used to gird yourself and walk wherever you wished; but when you grow old, you will stretch out your hands and someone else will gird you, and bring you where you do not wish to *go*." [19] Now this he said, signifying by what kind of death he would glorify God. And when he had spoken this, he said to him, "Follow Me!" (John 21:18–19)

How rare it is that we think of the kind of death by which we will glorify God.

We should expect suffering because we are

children of God, but our status as children of God should also cause us not to fear. Consider these encouraging words from John Willison:

> If in this world, then, we must look for tribulation, it is highly necessary for every man to seek direction how to provide for it, and behave under it, so as he may glorify God, edify others, and attain to eternal happiness at last. . . . These heavy trials are all needful for you. Deep waters are not more needful to carry a ship into the haven, than great afflictions are to carry the vessels of our souls into the port of bliss. Strong winds and thunder are frightful, but they are necessary to purge the air. . . . Consider that your affliction, however heavy it may be, will soon have an end. . . . The goldsmith will not let his gold lie longer in the furnace than it is purified. The wicked have a sea of wrath to drink; but, O drooping believer, take comfort; you have but a cup of affliction, which will soon be exhausted. . . . O believer, God hath taken the ordering of your lot in his own hand, and he knows what is fittest for you. . . . God sends great and sore troubles that you may have the more experience of God's wisdom and mercy in your support and deliverance. It is very ordinary for every man in great distress, to reckon his case singular, because he feels best what is nearest to himself, but is a stranger to

what his neighbor feels. . . . [But] whatever your case be, you must own your sufferings are not as great as your sins. If our provoked Judge shall, in his clemency, send us into Babylon instead of hell, we have no cause to complain.[19]

If you are a redeemed believer, then you have nothing to fear! You can be assured that the circumstances you face are given to you by God for a purpose. Therefore, trust him—believe him. As Calvin admonishes,

The believing heart does not haphazardly forge for itself some kind of god. Rather, it looks to him who is the true and only God. It does not ascribe to him whatever qualities it pleases but is content to take him as he shows himself to be; it is always careful not to depart from God's will through headstrong pride. Knowing him thus, and understanding that he governs all things by his providence, it confidently accepts him as guardian and protector, and therefore entrusts itself to his keeping, since it knows him to be the author of all that is good. If beset by pressing need, it at once falls back on him for help, and after calling on him by name it awaits his aid, for it is

---

[19] John Willison, "Directions to God's Children Under Affliction," in *Selections from Spurgeon's Library on Suffering* (Nashville: B&H Academic, 2018), 11–15.

persuaded that he is both generous and kind. It relies with assurance on his compassion, never doubting that for every distress there will be a remedy furnished by his mercy.[20]

So God ordained our suffering, but he also supplied us with the sufficient means to endure the suffering. The apostle Peter declares in 2 Peter 1:3a, "Seeing that his divine power has granted to us everything pertaining to life and godliness." The word *life* in that verse is a Greek noun that denotes life that is real and genuine, active and vigorous, devoted to God, and blessed by him, not only in the life to come, but even in this world. We cannot repeat this enough: we are convinced of the sufficiency of Scripture to address this issue of sinful fear and anxiety. We know this from Hebrews 4:12–13, which reads,

> For the word of God is living and active and sharper than any two-edged sword, and piercing as far as the division of soul and spirit, of both joints and marrow, and able to judge the thoughts and intentions of the heart. And there is no creature hidden from his sight, but all things

---

[20] John Calvin, *The Institutes of the Christian Religion*, ed. Robert White (Carlisle, PA: Banner of Truth, 2014), 8.

are open and laid bare to the eyes of him with whom we have to do.

That word *living* in Hebrews 4:12 is the verb form of the same Greek noun found in 2 Peter 1:3. The word *active* in verse 12 is the Greek noun from which we derive our English word *energy*. When Hebrews 4:12 speaks of God's Word being "living" and "active," it means precisely that. The Word of God isn't some static, dormant, lifeless, passive, or latent book that is comprised of mere words on a page. It is as the apostle Paul described it to the believers in the church at Thessalonica in 1 Thessalonians 2:13:

> For this reason we also constantly thank God that when you received the word of God which you heard from us, you accepted it not as the word of men, but for what it really is, the word of God, which performs its work in you who believe.

The reason Paul can say that the Word of God "performs its work" is because the Word of God is literally living and active. The Word of God is supernaturally imbued by the Spirit of God from whom the Word of God emanates, and it is made efficacious to "perform its work" in the hearts and minds of those who believe that Word. We see this divine vivification all the way back in Genesis 1:2: "The earth was formless and void, and darkness was over the surface of the deep, and the Spirit of God was moving over the surface of the waters." That the Scripture describes the Spirit of God as moving over the surface of the waters emphasizes that the Spirit of God is *animate* not inanimate; the Spirit of God is living and active, not dormant or passive.

So the Word of God is completely sufficient, as John Owen argued, "to help us to recover from our weaknesses." And as fallen and sinful human beings, we all have weaknesses. But thanks be to God that, as the writer of Hebrews says in Hebrews 4:15, "We do not have a high priest who cannot sympathize with our weaknesses, but one who has been tempted in all things as we are, yet without sin." For the believer in Jesus Christ, the first step to overcoming sinful fear and anxiety is to believe God and to trust in what he has said to us in his Word.

Consider this counsel from David Powlison:

Human beings instinctively oscillate between two sinful extremes. In the "objective" mode we typically deny feelings and so avoid the realities of interior life. Much of the time people are pragmatic, unreflective, driven by external pressures or by unstated demands, fears, and goals. In the "subjective" mode, on the other hand, we typically indulge feelings and so make feelings supreme. "Getting in touch with" denied feelings is the world's way of addressing one problem by creating another. The Holy Spirit and the Word of God set us free to live in a third way. This third way neither denies personal honesty nor equates truth with such honesty. You must pay attention to feelings! You must not live . . . as if feelings are the supreme reality. . . . The feeling of being overwhelmed often drives people to God, to self-evaluation, to seeking help. It also often sets people up for reacting via workaholism, suicide, anger, depression, drugs, or other escapisms. Is this feeling normative? No. It has a cause you need to discover and a "way of escape" you need to find because "God is faithful."[21]

The sad reality is that our culture currently worships at the altar of emotion, and as a result, feelings reign supreme. This is why we must reform our minds by Scripture so that we're not

---

[21] David Powlison, *Seeing with New Eyes: Counseling and the Human Condition Through the Lens of Scripture* (Phillipsburg, NJ: P & R Publishing, 2003), 220–21.

beholden to the emotion of our day.

Study Questions

1. Every person, whether or not he or she is a Christian, has a "theology of suffering" (p. 42). The only question is: Is their theology of suffering *biblical*? What is *your* theology of suffering? Could you articulate it if you were asked to? Prayerfully consider those questions in light of Philippians 1:29 and Romans 8:28. Commit both verses to memory.

2. Darrell and Virgil assert that it's important for Christians to, "always remember that our circumstances are primarily for the purpose of bringing glory to God" (p. 42). In what ways has that been the case for you?

3. How can reflecting on God's past faithfulness to you help you in those moments when you're feeling fearful and anxious?

4. Read Psalm 119:105 and commit it to memory. What does that verse teach concerning the sufficiency of Scripture and its capacity to guide, comfort, and counsel you? How can you practically apply the truths of that verse to your fight against sinful fear and anxiety?

5. Read and commit to memory 2 Thessalonians 3:3.

Will You Believe God's Word?

Christians should be incredibly thankful and humbled when we consider that our merciful and gracious God has left his people with his Word, the Holy Scriptures, which are altogether sufficient to help to us in navigating the waters of sinful fear and anxiety that we might experience living in this corrupt world. But the question you need to ask yourself is, do you believe that for yourself?

You see, we can walk through what the Word of God says about how to deal with sinful fear and anxiety, but you must believe God's Word for yourself. We can encourage and exhort you to believe the truths of God's Word, and yet the fact remains that believing God's Word is a decision you must make in your own mind and heart. We cannot make that decision for you. It's like the man in John 5:5–6 who had been ill for thirty-eight years; Jesus asked the man, "Do you wish to get well?"

Perhaps that question resonates with you: do you wish to get well? Do you truly desire to overcome sinful fear and anxiety in your life? If you are wavering in doubt and uncertainty about whether you can trust God and his Word in the particular situation in which you're feeling fearful and anxious, consider these encouraging yet sobering words of the apostle James in James 1:5–8, in which he gives us a promise, then a warning, then another promise. James writes:

> **Promise:** But if any of you lacks wisdom, let him ask of God, who gives to all generously and without reproach, and it will be given to him.

> **Warning:** But he must ask in faith without any doubting, for the one who doubts is like the surf of the sea, driven and tossed by the wind.

> **Promise:** For that man ought not to expect to receive anything from the Lord, being a double-minded man, unstable in all his ways.

Now, let's pair that passage with these words from Hebrews 11:6: "And without faith it is impossible to please him, for he who comes to God must believe that he is and that he is a rewarder of those who seek him." This brings to our minds the words of R. C. Sproul when he observes that there is a difference between believing *in* God and *believing* God.[22] Sproul expands on that in his commentary on the gospel of Luke:

> I don't think we take seriously enough the sinfulness of unbelief. We have a tendency in our culture, and even in the church, to think that belief in Christ or unbelief in Christ, believing and trusting in the things of God or not trusting in the things of God, are optional. They don't carry any dire consequences if we dismiss them. But we need to understand that unbelief in the Word of God is sin. And not only is it sin, but it's an egregious sin. And not only is it an egregious sin, but it's a sin that has eternal consequences.[23]

The writer of Hebrews is saying to us that it's not enough for us to merely come to God in the sense that we *believe* God exists—that's the easy part—but we must come to him in full expectation that he will graciously meet our needs. That's believing *in* God—and, admittedly, that's not always easy for finite and changeable sinners like us to do.

---

[22] R. C. Sproul, *Surprised by Suffering* (Wheaton, IL: Tyndale House Publishers, 1994), 113.
[23] R. C. Sproul, *Luke: An Expositional Commentary* (Orlando, FL: Ligonier Ministries, 2020), 13.

Consider this passage from Mark 6:1–6:

> He went away from there and came to his hometown, and his disciples followed him. And on the Sabbath he began to teach in the synagogue, and many who heard him were astonished, saying, "Where did this man get these things? What is the wisdom given to him? How are such mighty works done by his hands? Is not this the carpenter, the son of Mary and brother of James and Joses and Judas and Simon? And are not his sisters here with us?" And they took offense at him. And Jesus said to them, "A prophet is not without honor, except in his hometown and among his relatives and in his own household." And he could do no mighty work there, except that he laid his hands on a few sick people and healed them. And he marveled because of their unbelief.

That word *marveled* in this passage is a Greek verb that means that Jesus wasn't simply puzzled at their unbelief, as if he were curious as to why the people didn't believe he was the Messiah. No, it means that Jesus was astonished at their unbelief, so much so that he performed no great miracles right there in his own hometown.

Our point is this: Jesus had "many listeners," but not many believers. If you're a professing Christian, what you must understand is that nothing we have written here will do you any good whatsoever in your struggling with sinful fear and anxiety apart from your willingness to believe the Word of God for yourself.

As the psalmist asks, introspectively, in Psalm 43:5, "Why are you in despair, O my soul? And why are you disturbed within me? Hope in God, for I shall again praise him, the help of my countenance and my God." And if Psalm 43:5 happens to not be where you are attitudinally right now, then, we urge you to not be ashamed to pray as the man did in Mark 9:24: "Lord, I believe. Help my unbelief." As the great English nineteenth-century minister, J. C. Ryle says,

> There are degrees of grace and degrees of faith. Those who have most faith and grace will have most happiness. But all, more or less, compared to the children of the world, are happy men. Do I say that real true Christians are equally happy at all times? No, not for a moment! All have their ebbs and flows of comfort. . . . Their bodily health is not always the same; their earthly circumstances are not always the same; the souls of those they love fill them at seasons with special

anxiety; they themselves are sometimes overtaken by a fault, and walk in darkness. They sometimes give way to inconsistencies and besetting sins, and lose their sense of pardon. But, as a general rule, the true Christian has a deep pool of peace within him, which even at the lowest is never entirely dry. . . . The true Christian is the only happy man because he has sources of happiness entirely independent of this world. He has something which cannot be affected by sickness and by deaths, by private losses and by public calamities — the "peace of God which passes all understanding." He has a hope laid up for him in heaven; he has a treasure which moth and rust cannot corrupt; he has a house which can never be taken down. His loving wife may die, and his heart feel torn in two; his darling children may be taken from him, and he may be left alone in this cold world; his earthly plans may be crossed; his health may fail: but all this time he has a portion which nothing can hurt. He has one Friend who never dies; he has possessions beyond the grave, of which nothing can deprive him. . . . This is real happiness.[24]

---

[24] J. C. Ryle, *Practical Religion* (Carlisle, PA: Banner of Truth, 2013), 234–35.

Study Questions

1. Read John 5:1–6, Romans 6:6, and 1 Thessalonians 2:13 and answer, honestly: Do you believe that God's Word, as His Word is appropriated to your heart and mind by the power of the Holy Spirit, is able to "make you well" and to free you from your enslavement to sinful fear and anxiety?

2. Read 2 Timothy 2:20–21, Ephesians 2:10, and Philippians 2:13. How should knowing that God both ordains *and* uses your circumstances to make you "prepared for every good work" encourage you, particularly in light of His desire to make you more like Christ?

3. Read Matthew 13:53–58, Mark 6:1–6, and Hebrews 11:6. What do those passages teach about the role belief — and unbelief — in God and in His Word plays in your struggle with sinful fear and anxiety?

4. Commit Hebrews 11:6 to memory.

5. What are some ways you are committed to demonstrate faith instead of fear in a particular circumstance?

The True Source of Peace

We would not have written this book if we weren't thoroughly convinced of the sufficiency and efficacy of the Scriptures to profitably address our needs. But therein lies the rub when it comes to this matter of sinful fear and anxiety: many professing Christians simply do not believe God's Word is sufficient to help them in the areas of their life. They're seeking counsel, guidance, direction, and even peace from everywhere and from everyone but God and his Word. Every professing Christian would confess that they believe *in* God, but unfortunately many of those same professing Christians often fail to confess that they *believe* God. Doubt is the soil in which the roots of sinful fear and anxiety grow deep and bear much fruit.

Charles Haddon Spurgeon had these penetrating words to say about doubt in a sermon he preached on August 18, 1889, titled "Faith Essential to Pleasing God":

> Some of you are always fashioning fresh nets of doubt for your own entanglement. You invent snares for your own feet, and are greedy to lay more and more of them. You are mariners who

seek the rocks, soldiers who court the point of the bayonet. It is an unprofitable business. Practically, mentally, morally, spiritually, doubting is an evil trade. You are like a [black]smith, wearing out his arm in making chains with which to bind himself. Doubt is sterile, a desert without water. Doubt discovers difficulties which it never solves: it creates hesitancy, despondency, and despair.[25]

Job understood the importance of trusting God amid tragedy. Job not only believed *in* God, he *believed* God. That's why he was able to say in the midst of everything that was going on around him—even though he didn't have a clue as to why, "Though he slay me, I will hope in him" (Job 13:15a).

Remember, there is a difference between believing in God and believing God, and that can mean the difference between living in victory and living in defeat. The apostle Paul says in Ephesians 2:14 that Jesus "is our peace," and Jesus promises us in John 14:27, "Peace I leave with you; My peace I give to you; not as the

---

[25] C. H. Spurgeon, "Faith Essential to Pleasing God," in *The Metropolitan Tabernacle Pulpit Sermons*, vol. 35 (London: Passmore & Alabaster, 1889), 455.

world gives do I give to you. Do not let your heart be troubled, nor let it be fearful."

We don't often consider that the second half of that verse in John 14:27 is a command. *Do not let* your heart be troubled. That is a command of our Lord to us, his people, that we can choose either to obey or disobey— regardless of the situation or circumstance in which we find ourselves. It's as if Jesus is saying to us that if your heart is troubled, it's because you've let it be troubled, you've allowed it to be disturbed. And that's because you've taken the eyes of your mind and heart off him and put them onto the things which you've allowed your flesh, with its mercurial feelings and emotions, to be centered upon (Col 3:1–3).

The command is this: Do not let your heart be troubled. There is no asterisk in that verse pointing you to some fine print elsewhere in God's Word that says it's okay to allow your heart to be troubled in this situation or in that circumstance. No, there is no fine print to be found. Remember, it was Jesus himself in Matthew 11:28–29 who said, "Come unto me, all who are weary and heavy-laden, and I will give you rest. Take My yoke upon you and learn from me, for I am gentle and humble in heart, and you will find rest for your souls."

Think about those words. What is it that the person who is struggling with sinful fear and anxiety fundamentally wants most for themselves? What they want most is rest for their souls. But the rest they so desperately seek is found in Jesus Christ, and in him only. Jesus said in John 16:33, "These things I have spoken to you so that in me you may have peace. In the world you have tribulation, but take courage; I have overcome the world."

Nineteenth-century Scottish churchman Horatius Bonar observed:

> The counteraction of all fear, the removal of all doubt, comes from the knowledge of Christ himself. "Then were the disciples glad—when they saw the Lord." He spoke peace to his apostle John by reminding him of who and what he was and is. So does he still speak to us—nor will one fear ever be dispelled, or one doubt removed, in any other way. The sight of Christ will do everything—no other sight will do anything. A simpler, fuller knowledge of this gracious One is all that we need to give us perfect peace, and to keep

us in that peace forever![26]

Bonar said the sight of Christ will do everything—no other sight will do anything. Those sentiments are reflected in the beloved hymn "Be Still, My Soul," written in 1752 by the eighteenth-century German hymnwriter Catharina von Schlegel:

Be still, my soul: the Lord is on thy side;
bear patiently the cross of grief or pain;
leave to thy God to order and provide;
in ev'ry change he faithful will remain.
Be still, my soul: thy best, thy heav'nly Friend
through thorny ways leads to a joyful end.

Jesus said "in Me" you have peace, not in your hobbies, not in your best friends, not in your parents, or your job, or your bank account, or your vacation home, or your educational accomplishments, or your social media followers, or your psychiatrist or counselor, not even in your husband or your wife or your church for that matter. Peace is found only in Jesus Christ because only Jesus Christ *is* peace!

---

[26] Horatius Bonar, *The Revelation of Jesus Christ* (New York: Robert Carter & Brothers, 1872), 69.

If you're looking for peace anywhere or in anyone other than in Jesus Christ, you're engaged in a never-ending exercise in futility, because you're not going to find it. As John MacArthur explains,

> Godly peace has nothing to do with human beings or human circumstances. In fact, godly peace cannot be produced on a human level at all. Any peace that can be produced by humans is very fragile. It can be destroyed instantly by failure, doubt, fear, difficulty, guilt, shame, distress, sorrow, the anxiety of making the wrong choice, the anticipation of being mistreated or victimized by someone, the uncertainty of the future, and any challenge to our position or possessions. And we experience these things daily. The peace that God gives is not subject to the vicissitudes of life. It is a spiritual peace; it is an attitude of heart and mind when we believe and thus know deep down that all is well between ourselves and God. Along with it is the assurance that he is lovingly in control of everything. We as Christians should know for sure that our sins are forgiven, that God is concerned with our well-being, and that heaven is our destiny.[27]

---

[27] John MacArthur, *Anxious for Nothing: God's Cure for the Cares of Your Soul* (Ontario: David C Cook, 2012), 106.

A prime example of finding peace in the proper source, even amidst tragedy, is what happened in the life of Horatio Spafford, who tragically lost his son to scarlet fever and much of his business during the Chicago fire of 1871. Spafford sent his wife and four daughters on a trip across the Atlantic, planning to follow them soon. The ship was involved in a collision, and more than 200 people died, including Horatio Spafford's daughters. Horatio's wife sent word back to him via telegram, saying "Saved alone, what shall I do." Horatio boarded a boat to join his wife, and during the trip, he was told of the place where his daughters and hundreds of others died. Sometime thereafter, he penned the words to a familiar hymn:

> When peace, like a river, attendeth my way,
> when sorrows like sea billows roll;
> whatever my lot,
> Thou hast taught me to say,
> It is well, it is well with my soul.
>
> Though Satan should buffet,
> though trials should come,
> let this blest assurance control,
> that Christ hath regarded my helpless estate,
> and hath shed his own blood for my soul.

My sin, oh the bliss of this glorious thought!
my sin, not in part but the whole,
is nailed to his cross, and I bear it no more!
Praise the Lord, praise the Lord, O my soul!

And Lord haste the day,
when the faith shall be sight,
the clouds be rolled back as a scroll;
the trump shall resound,
and the Lord shall descend!
Even so, it is well with my soul.

Horatio reunited with his wife, and they had two more children, never replacing those who were lost, but allowing the next generation to see the glory of God in how they responded to tragedy.

When we face tragedy or difficult circumstances, we must, like Spafford, trust God and believe his promises. At the end of the day, having victory over sinful fear and anxiety really boils down to who you are going to trust as the true source of peace.

Are you going to allow the Scripture to be sufficient to calm your soul?

Study Questions

1. Horatius Bonar said, "The counteraction of all fear, the removal of all doubt, comes from the knowledge of Christ himself" (p. 62). Is there anything—or anyone—in your life today that has replaced the Lord Jesus Christ as your source of peace? If so, write them down, along with the specific ways in which they have served as substitutes for Christ as your source of peace.

2. John MacArthur said, "Godly peace has nothing to do with human beings or human circumstances" (p. 64). Consider that statement in light of Jesus's words in John 16:33. How should the reality that Jesus overcame the world encourage you in overcoming your struggle with sinful fear and anxiety?

3. Read and commit to memory Psalm 4:8.

4. Read and commit to memory Psalm 55:22.

5. In what ways does meditation on the two previous verses help to overcome fear?

Let the Peace of Christ Rule Your Heart

Here's the simple truth: the cure for sinful fear and anxiety is a heart-centered trust in God and in his infallible and inerrant Word.

This is true regardless of whether the fear and anxiety you're dealing with right now has to do with something that occurred today or in the past. Consider what Steve Viars says for those who may be dealing with fear and anxiety because of their past:

> What was God thinking? He could have made us without the capacity to remember. Every day would literally be a new day with no memories, no past, and no baggage. Would that make life better? If you could walk through a device similar to a metal detector at an airport but one that would erase your past and its effects on you today, would you do it? And would you be better off? Some people seem to think so. They describe the past with phrases such as "toxic past," "wounded inner child," or "damaged emotions." In many cases they do so with good reason. . . . But does that mean that the past, in its entirety, is a bad thing? Would we all be better off if we

could completely erase our memories and the impact our past has on our lives today? Not if we allow God's Word to guide us. The Bible gives us several ways our past can be among our best friends. Of course your past is not an "it." It is not a separate entity. But it is a record, in part, of the way God has related to you and worked in your life. The goal is not to focus on "it" but on who God is and what he has done.[28]

In Mark 11:22, Jesus encouraged Peter and the other disciples to, "have faith in God." Jesus wasn't talking about a blind faith in God, but the kind of faith of which the apostle John speaks of in 1 John 4:4: "You are from God, little children, and have overcome them; because greater is he who is in you than he who is in the world." And as 1 John 5:4-5 states, "For whatever is born of God overcomes the world; and this is the victory that has overcome the world — our faith. Who is the one who overcomes the world, but he who believes that Jesus is the Son of God?"

Each of us has been sinfully afraid and fearful at one point or another. To deny that would

[28] Stephen Viars, *Putting Your Past in Its Place: Moving Forward in Freedom and Forgiveness* (Eugene, OR: Harvest House Publishers, 2011), 47-48.

be to deny our very humanity. As redeemed sinners who have been sinfully fearful ourselves, we are simply trying to point other redeemed sinners—and even *unredeemed* sinners—to the one in whom they *can* trust in those moments when they're feeling overwhelmed by thoughts and feelings of fear and anxiety.

As the psalmist writes in Psalm 94:17–19:

> If the Lord had not been my help, my soul would soon have dwelt in the abode of silence. If I should say, "My foot has slipped," your lovingkindness, O Lord, will hold me up. When my anxious thoughts multiply within me, Your consolations delight my soul.

And 1 Peter 5:6–7 states:

> Therefore humble yourselves under the mighty hand of God, that he may exalt you at the proper time, casting all your anxiety on him, because he cares for you.

And speaking of God's care for his people, read these reassuring words by John Flavel:

> Learn to quench all slavish creature-fears in the reverential fear of God. This is a cure by

diversion. It is an exercise of Christian wisdom to turn those passions of the soul which most predominate, into spiritual channels; to turn natural anger into spiritual zeal, natural mirth into holy cheerfulness, and natural fear into a holy dread and awe of God. This method of cure, Christ prescribes in the 10th chapter of Matthew; similar to which is Isaiah, 8:12–13, "Fear not their fear." 'But how shall we help it?' "Sanctify the Lord of hosts himself; and let him be your fear, and let him be your dread." Natural fear may be allayed for the present by natural reason, or the removal of the occasion; but then it is like a candle blown out by a puff of breath, which is easily blown in again: but if the fear of God extinguish it, then it is like a candle quenched in water, which cannot easily be rekindled. Pour out to God in prayer those fears which the devil and your own unbelief pour in upon you in times of danger. Prayer is the best outlet to fear: where is the Christian that cannot set his seal to this direction? I will give you the greatest example to encourage you to compliance, even the example of Jesus Christ. When the hour of his danger and death drew nigh, he went into the garden, separated from his disciples, and there wrestled mightily with God in prayer, even unto agony; in reference to which the apostle says, "who in the days of his flesh, when he had offered up prayers and supplications, with strong cries and tears, to him that was able to save from death, and was heard in that he feared." He was heard as to strength and support to carry him through it; though not as to deliverance, or exemption from it. O that these things may abide with you, and be reduced to practice in these evil days, and that many trembling may be established by them.[29]

We would like to leave you with this admonition from the apostle Paul in Colossians 3:15–16 as application: "Let the peace of Christ rule in your hearts. . . . Let the Word of Christ richly dwell within you."

When you consistently obey those two commands, you'll have no legitimate reason to be fearful or anxious about anything. Finally, we exhort you to prayerfully consider these encouraging words from Michael S. Lundy:

> Do not overlook the miracle of love that God has shown us in the wonderful incarnation, office, life, death, resurrection, ascension, and reign of our Redeemer. Rather, steep your thoughts most of all in these wonders of mercy, ordained by

---

[29] John Flavel, *A Treatise on the Keeping of the Heart* (New Brunswick, NJ: A. Blauvelt, 1801), 84.

God to be the primary substance of your thoughts. You should rationally bring to mind many thoughts about Christ and grace for each one you list about your sin and misery, but in a manner that tends to magnify the remedy and to cause you to embrace it.[30]

"Now may the God of hope fill you with all joy and peace in believing, so that you will abound in hope by the power of the Holy Spirit." — Romans 15:13

Study Questions

1. Read and commit to memory John 14:1. What is it today that so concerns you that you're allowing your heart to be "troubled"? How does allowing your heart to be troubled rob you of the kind of peace that Jesus desires you to have?

---

[30] J. I. Packer, *Depression, Anxiety, and the Christian Life: Practical Wisdom from Richard Baxter*, ed. Michael S. Lundy (Wheaton, IL: Crossway, 2018), 91.

2. What is the relationship between Jesus's command in John 14:1 to "not let your heart be troubled" and His commands in Matthew 6:25–34 to "not worry"?

3. John Flavel said that Christians should "learn to quench all slavish creature-fears in the reverential fear of God" (p. 72). What is the relationship between Flavel's words and those of the apostle Paul in 2 Corinthians 10:5, to "take every thought captive to the obedience of Christ"?

4. Read and commit to memory John 14:27.

5. Based upon what we've read and studied, what will you do when fear arises in your mind?

For Further Reading

Bennett, Arthur, ed. *The Valley of Vision: A Collection of Puritan Prayers & Devotions*. Carlisle, PA: Banner of Truth, 1975.

Bonar, Horatius. *The Revelation of Jesus Christ*. New York: Robert Carter & Brothers, 1872.

Boston, Thomas. *Human Nature in Its Fourfold State*. Glasgow: J. & M. Robertson, 1794.

Bridges, Jerry. *Trusting God*. Colorado Springs: NavPress, 2017.

Caldwell, Richard. *Answering Anxiety: A Biblical Answer for What Troubles Your Heart*. The Woodlands, TX: Kress Christian Publications, 2017.

Flavel, John. *A Treatise on the Keeping of the Heart*. New Brunswick, NJ: A. Blauvelt, 1801.

Flavel, John. *Triumphing Over Sinful Fear*. Grand Rapids: Reformation Heritage Books, 2011.

Gurnall, William. *The Christian in Complete Armour*. Carlisle, PA: Banner of Truth, 1964.

MacArthur, John. *Anxious for Nothing: God's Cure for the Cares of Your Soul*. Ontario: David C Cook, 2012.

Owen, John. *Searching Our Hearts in Difficult Times*. Carlisle, PA: Banner of Truth, 2019.

Packer, J. I. *Depression, Anxiety, and the Christian Life: Practical Wisdom from Richard Baxter*. Edited by Michael S. Lundy. Wheaton, IL: Crossway, 2018.

Powlison, David. *How Does Sanctification Work?* Wheaton, IL: Crossway, 2017.

Powlison, David. *Seeing with New Eyes: Counseling and the Human Condition Through the Lens of Scripture*. Phillipsburg, NJ: P & R Publishing, 2003.

Priolo, Lou. *Fear: Breaking Its Grip*. Phillipsburg, NJ: P & R Publishing, 2009.

Ryle, J. C. *Practical Religion*. Carlisle, PA: Banner of Truth, 2013.

Scott, Stuart. *Anger, Anxiety, and Fear: A Biblical Perspective*. Bemidji, MN: Focus Publishing, 2009.

Sibbes, Richard. *The Bruised Reed*. Carlisle, PA: Banner of Truth, 1998.

Sproul, R. C. *Surprised by Suffering*. Wheaton, IL: Tyndale House Publishers, 1994.

Sproul, Jr., R. C. *Believing God*. Lake Mary, FL: Reformation Trust Publishing, 2009.

Spurgeon, C. H. "Faith Essential to Pleasing God." In *The Metropolitan Tabernacle Pulpit Sermons*, Vol. 35. London: Passmore & Alabaster, 1889.

Troxel, A. Craig. *With All Your Heart: Orienting Your Mind, Desires, and Will toward Christ.* Wheaton, IL: Crossway, 2020.

Viars, Stephen. *Putting Your Past in Its Place: Moving Forward in Freedom and Forgiveness.* Eugene, OR: Harvest House Publishers, 2011.

Welch, Edward T. *Running Scared: Fear, Worry, and the God of Rest.* Greensboro, NC: New Growth Press, 2007.

Willison, John. "Directions to God's Children Under Affliction." In *Selections from Spurgeon's Library on Suffering.* Nashville: B&H Academic, 2018.

For more helpful resources
that encourage, equip, and educate the church,
visit **www.G3Min.org.**